T0023834

MRS AND MRS

Compiled by Eve Willis

An Hachette UK Company
www.hachette.co.uk

Summersdale Publishers Ltd
Part of Octopus Publishing Group Limited
Carmelite House
50 Victoria Embankment
LONDON
EC4Y 0DZ
UK

www.summersdale.com

Printed and bound in China

ISBN: 978-1-80007-174-2

Substantial discounts on bulk quantities of Summersdale books are available to corporations, professional associations and other organizations. For details contact general enquiries: telephone: +44 (0) 1243 771107 or email: enquiries@summersdale.com.

To..

From..

Each time
you love, love
as deeply as
if it were
FOREVER.

AUDRE LORDE

I didn't know
how to not
be with her.

TIG NOTARO

LOVE
IS THE
ANSWER

I JUST MISS YOU,
IN A QUITE SIMPLE
DESPERATE HUMAN
WAY... IT IS
incredible
HOW ESSENTIAL TO
ME YOU HAVE BECOME.

VITA SACKVILLE-WEST

Fear should not get in the way of how you love or who you love.

JANELLE MONÁE

You shall have
every smile and
every breath
of tenderness.

ANNE LISTER

MY HEART
CHOOSES YOU

Women are
beautiful, strong and
compassionate.

RITA MAE BROWN

Oh it puts the
heart in my chest
on wings for when
I look at you,
even a moment,
no speaking is
left in me.

SAPPHO

YOU'RE MY FAVOURITE EVERYTHING

♥

The two of them
grew stronger
together every
day... Together
they possessed
a miracle.

PATRICIA HIGHSMITH

She reached and took my hand. She took it, not to be led by me, not to be comforted; only to hold it, because it was mine.

SARAH WATERS

YOU ARE

one of my
nicest thoughts.

GEORGIA O'KEEFFE

LIFE IS TOO SHORT TO DENY LOVE

When she lowers
her eyes, she seems
to hold all the beauty
in the world between
her eyelids; when she
raises them, I see only
myself in her gaze.

NATALIE CLIFFORD BARNEY

Funny was that
I couldn't say
je t'aime and *je
t'adore* as I longed
to do, but always
remember that
I am saying it,
that I go to sleep
thinking of you.

ELEANOR ROOSEVELT

LOVE
HAS NO
GENDER

BUT THIS IS ANOTHER
LOVE — IT GOES

THERE IS NO PLACE
FOR IT TO STOP.

DJUNA BARNES

Perhaps we were friends first and lovers second. But then perhaps this is what lovers are.

ANDRÉ ACIMAN

LOVE:

the skilful
audacity
required to
share an
inner life.

GERTRUDE STEIN

I LOVE YOU
IN EVERY
LANGUAGE

Everybody should be allowed to be who they are, and to love who they love.

DOLLY PARTON

IT IS SO EASY LOVING YOU

Marriage
ISN'T BETWEEN A
MAN AND WOMAN,
BUT BETWEEN
LOVE AND LOVE.

FRANK OCEAN

I love you with
a love that
surpasses that
of friendship...
were I to embrace
you with all that
remains of me.

GERMAINE DE STAËL

I'm married to my best friend and nothing has ever brought me more joy than that.

BRANDI CARLILE

I BELONG
WITH YOU

There's happiness, and then there's love and then there's completion.

ELLEN DeGENERES

Falling in love
with my wife
was one of the
great delights
and surprises
of my life.

CYNTHIA NIXON

In your eyes
I see myself
become what
I always

DREAMED

I could be.

ISABEL MILLER

YOU MAKE MY HEART SMILE

It's a matter of suddenly, globally, "knowing" that another person represents your only access to some vitally transmissible truth.

EVE KOSOFSKY SEDGWICK
ON FALLING IN LOVE

Life is... breathtaking with you.

SAMIRA WILEY TO LAUREN MORELLI

Getting to choose you every day is the best thing.

LAUREN MORELLI TO SAMIRA WILEY

YOU WILL
FOREVER BE
MY ALWAYS

I have learned
not to worry
about love, but
to honour its
coming with
all my heart.

ALICE WALKER

What I would
like most of all
is to be in a state
of blissful love.

FREDDIE MERCURY

I LOVE
BEING YOURS

When you put love out in the world it travels, and it can touch people... in ways that we never even expected.

LAVERNE COX

One is loved
because
one is loved.
No reason is
needed for
LOVING.

PAULO COELHO

To be fully seen by somebody, then, and be loved anyhow — this is a human offering that can border on miraculous.

ELIZABETH GILBERT

LOVE MAKES
US RICHER

The things we truly love stay with us always, locked in our hearts as long as life remains.

JOSEPHINE BAKER

THE MOST POWERFUL
WEAPON ON EARTH
IS THE HUMAN
soul on fire.

FERDINAND FOCH

YOU
FEEL
LIKE
HOME

Instead of disappearing, she makes me feel reappeared. Reimagined. Her touch shapes me, draws out the boldness that had been hiding in my core.

NATASHA NGAN

I saw somebody and [experienced] all of those things you hear about in songs and read about in poetry.

PORTIA DE ROSSI

Love is
friendship
that has
caught fire.

ANN LANDERS

WHEN I MET YOU, I FOUND ME

*I think of you daily,
and am always
devotedly yours.*

OSCAR WILDE

When I left I thought, "I have just met [my] life."

FIONA SHAW ON FIRST
MEETING HER WIFE

IT ONLY TOOK A HEARTBEAT TO FALL FOR YOU

♥

People fall in love with people, not gender, not looks... What I'm in love with exists on almost a spiritual level.

MILEY CYRUS

The important
thing is not
the object of
love, but the
EMOTION
itself.

GORE VIDAL

All love
THAT HAS NOT
FRIENDSHIP FOR
ITS BASE IS LIKE
A MANSION BUILT
UPON SAND.

ELLA WHEELER WILCOX

I CAN DO
ANYTHING
WITH YOU
NEXT TO ME

She appeared
out of nowhere
and it felt like
I'd known
her forever.

FORTUNE FEIMSTER

There are a
hundred paths
through the world
that are easier
than loving. But,
who wants easier?

MARY OLIVER

Every moment is
made glorious by
the light of love.

RUMI

When we love
we can let our
hearts speak.

BELL HOOKS

Where there
is love there is
LIFE.

MAHATMA GANDHI

LOVE
IS LOVE

I was not born
to live alone.
I must have the
object with me
and in loving
and being loved,
I could be happy.

ANNE LISTER

YOU MAKE MY
SOUL SING

♥

IT'S ALWAYS WRONG TO HATE,

but it's never wrong to love.

LADY GAGA

I ache to hold
you close.

ELEANOR ROOSEVELT

I think it is high
time to tell you
that I think of
you constantly.

MARLENE DIETRICH

Love is composed of a single soul inhabiting two bodies.

ARISTOTLE

YOU MADE
ME POSSIBLE

I don't believe in luck often but how lucky am I that you chose me. I love you for all of our chapters and the forever, "to be continued" endings.

KRISTEN KISH

I can live without money, but I cannot live without love.

JUDY GARLAND

How lucky I am to have found what romance novels call

"MY OTHER HALF".

SANDI TOKSVIG

The freedom of being out and open about who I am allowed me to find and fall in love with... the most amazing woman I've ever known.

CHELY WRIGHT

I love [her]
so much it's
painful. She's
my best friend.

QUINN WILSON

I ADORE YOU

Love is
A HUMAN
EXPERIENCE,
NOT A POLITICAL
STATEMENT.

ANNE HATHAWAY

Nothing is mysterious, no human relation. Except love.

SUSAN SONTAG

YOUR LOVE IS THE SWEETEST I HAVE EVER KNOWN

♥

Now I know
the meaning
of life is love.

CARA DELEVINGNE

If we have the opportunity to be generous with our hearts, ourselves, we have no idea of the depth and breadth of love's reach.

MARGARET CHO

For you are the essence of the stars and the moon and the mystery of the night.

MERCEDES DE ACOSTA

YOU ARE MY
TODAY AND
ALL OF MY
TOMORROWS

In the passage of their lives together... every item in the house, every word they spoke, attested to their mutual love, the combining of their humours.

DJUNA BARNES

**You are, I think,
an evening star,
the fairest of
all the stars.**

SAPPHO

I LOVE YOU.
ALWAYS HAVE,
ALWAYS WILL

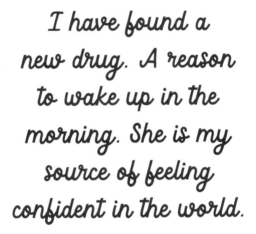

I have found a
new drug. A reason
to wake up in the
morning. She is my
source of feeling
confident in the world.

CHLOE CALDWELL

But you
have broken
down my
DEFENCES.
And I don't
really resent it.

VITA SACKVILLE-WEST
TO VIRGINIA WOOLF

In case you ever
foolishly forget:
I am never not
thinking of you.

VIRGINIA WOOLF TO
VITA SACKVILLE-WEST

LOVE
CONQUERS
ALL

*I had to be
with her,*
AND I JUST FIGURED
I'D DEAL WITH THE
OTHER STUFF LATER.

PORTIA DE ROSSI

I didn't want to live a life without love.

EDIE WINDSOR

WHEN I AM WITH YOU, THE WHOLE WORLD STOPS

♥

There are different levels of being in love with someone, and maybe everyone doesn't find that undeniable, indescribable... I can't describe it, it's indescribable.

KRISTEN STEWART

Love has nothing to do with what you are expecting to get — only with what you are expecting to give — which is everything.

KATHARINE HEPBURN

I love you
MORE THAN
LIFE ITSELF.

LENA WAITHE

LET'S GROW OLD TOGETHER

I knew we'd
cross paths
someday – I just
wasn't quite sure
when or how.

EMMA PORTNER

Love is the emblem of eternity.

GERMAINE DE STAËL

I NEED
YOU LIKE
THE AIR I
BREATHE

We are one now...
and that's the
greatest gift.

LINDA PERRY

No one is
more deeply
GRATEFUL
that you were
born than I.

SARAH PAULSON

Having you by my side is a gift as we continue to navigate this thing called life.

AMBER LAIGN

YOU ARE
MY SUNSHINE
ON THE
RAINIEST DAYS

AND I TELL YOU,
IN TWO MINUTES, I FELL
in love with her.

LILY TOMLIN

Your heart knows the way. Run in that direction.

RUMI

A LIST OF REASONS I LOVE YOU:

1. YOU'RE YOU

♥

Every day I'm
a proud wife.

ALEXANDRA HEDISON

The deep intimacy of being two people talking about the core of who we are. Talking about our journeys... That's how we fell in love.

SAMIRA WILEY

It was an ecstatic time when we found each other.

JANE WAGNER

WHAT WOULD I DO WITHOUT YOU?

I am that
clumsy human,
always loving,
loving, loving.
And loving.

FRIDA KAHLO

If love will not swing wide the gates, no other **POWER** will or can.

JAMES BALDWIN

WHEN YOU PUT YOUR ARMS AROUND ME I AM HOME

Once you follow your heart, it's all of a sudden so easy.

STEPHANIE ALLYNNE

PEOPLE SHOULD *fall in love* WITH THEIR EYES CLOSED. JUST CLOSE YOUR EYES. DON'T LOOK AND IT'S MAGIC.

ANDY WARHOL

When you love someone, you are sure. You don't need time to decide... You know the immensity of what you have, and you protect it.

NINA LACOUR

Be a lover.
Give love.
Choose love.

HARRY STYLES

Just be open,
honest and
always have
your love's
best interest
AT HEART.

CHERRY JONES

LET OUR
LOVE SHINE
FOR ALL THE
WORLD TO SEE

♥

I never knew
I could find
someone that
matches me the
way she does, in
all ways... always.

HEATHER TURMAN ON
HEATHER MATARAZZO

To death and
back, I love you.

HEATHER MATARAZZO
TO HEATHER TURMAN

Love is the thing we
were created for.

NIECY NASH

NOTHING COMPARES TO MY LOVE FOR YOU

Whenever there's a question, she goes:

"THE ANSWER'S LOVE."

LINDA WALLEM ON
MELISSA ETHERIDGE

Love has a
way of coming...
It found its way
into my home.

MELISSA ETHERIDGE

IN THE END, LOVE IS THE ONLY THING THAT MATTERS

WHOA! NOW
I GET IT...
I get why
PEOPLE WRITE SONGS.

BEANIE FELDSTEIN
ON MEETING HER GIRLFRIEND

"One shall our union and our interests be" and every wish that love inspires and every kiss and every dear feeling of delight shall only make me more securely and entirely yours.

ANNE LISTER

It's a short ride on this earth, spend your time with someone that inspires you to be the best version of yourself.

DYLAN MEYER

YOU
MAKE
ME FEEL
SPECIAL

I feel joyful with her every single day... The joy is just being who I am with my girlfriend every single day.

MADISON BAILEY

We were together – all else has long been forgotten by me.

WALT WHITMAN

MY HEART
WANTS
ONLY YOU

♥

It was just immediately like, "Oh, this is home."

MEGAN RAPINOE
ON MEETING HER PARTNER

I just knew. I just knew and so did she. I've never smiled as much as I have this last year.

MARIA BELLO

Thus love
HAS THE MAGIC
POWER TO MAKE OF
A BEGGAR A KING.

EMMA GOLDMAN

TOGETHER, WE CAN DO ANYTHING

Take all my
love — now and
FOR EVER.

OSCAR WILDE

We're all unique and beautiful in our own way and entitled to love and be loved by whomever we choose.

BARBRA STREISAND

When I see her...
It's like I never
saw anything at all
before. It's like I
am filling up, like a
wine glass when it's
filled with wine.

SARAH WATERS

I got married to a woman who understands me from trigger to joy, from breakfast to midnight snack, from stage to home.

RAVEN-SYMONÉ

I love you with so much of my heart that none is left to protest.

WILLIAM SHAKESPEARE

You came and I was
longing for you.
You cooled a
heart that burned
with desire.

SAPPHO

OUR LOVE IS TOO BEAUTIFUL TO HIDE IN A CLOSET

♥

LOVE
doesn't cease;
love reshapes.

—————————

IMAN

ONE WORD UNITES ALL OF US: LOVE

Love demands expression... It will break out in tongues of praise, the high note that smashes the glass and spills the liquid.

JEANETTE WINTERSON

She was someone who listened to me, she took [care] of what I said, who listened to my anger, and together, mobile, we faced life, we rose up.

ADÉLE HAENEL

NOTHING EVER TRULY MADE SENSE UNTIL YOU *came into my life.*

MARIAH LINNEY

You will always
be my reason to
believe in that
soul-hugging
kind of love.

KRISTEN KISH

When she kissed her, her mouth as warm as summer, the taste of her sweet and clear, she knew, at last, that she was home.

MALINDA LO

Have you enjoyed this book? If so, find us on Facebook at **Summersdale Publishers**, on Twitter at **@Summersdale** and on Instagram at **@summersdalebooks** and get in touch. We'd love to hear from you!

www.summersdale.com